Still He speaks to those walking the beaches of life.

MW00999490

Three times beside the sea
the Lord spoke to me
in parables.
He led me first to . . .

The Parable of the

Shell

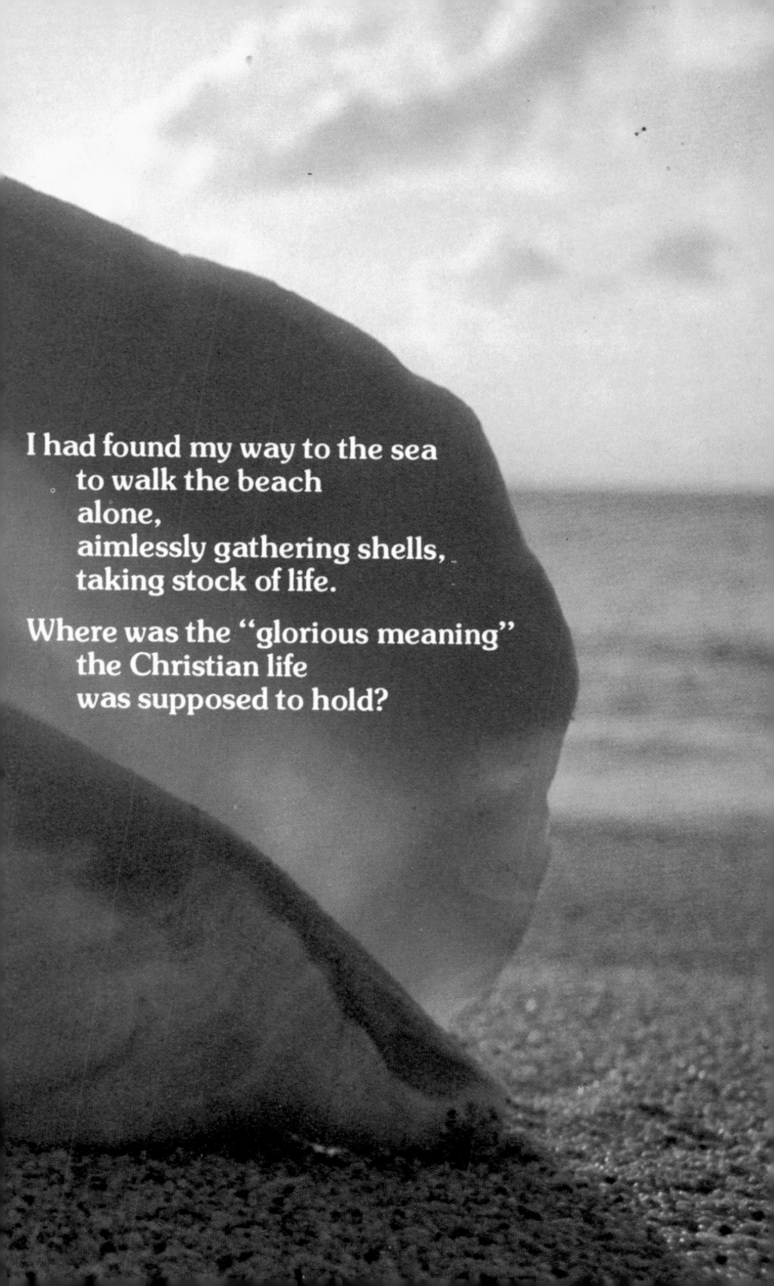

I had found my way to the sea
to walk the beach
alone,
aimlessly gathering shells,
taking stock of life.

Where was the "glorious meaning"
the Christian life
was supposed to hold?

Life?
　This barren,
　bleak,
　empty existence?
　Footprints leading nowhere.

For me, life was like the beach—
    a tossed-up pile of driftwood,
    a monotonous stretch of sand,
    a tide rushing in, ebbing out,
    endlessly,
    meaninglessly.
Have you been there?

A shell caught my eye,
    a shape unfamiliar,
    etched with an exquisitely
    delicate pattern,
    pricked with a fine needle,
    brushed with a hint of color.
The work of a beach artist?
But why had he tossed it away?
    What waste!

Another shell.
    I was startled.
    The same delicate pattern,
    the same soft color.
And another!

I laughed,
    recognizing at last
    the Artist's signature:
        GOD

Then I heard Him in the winds
    telling me
    the Parable of the Shell:
"If I have a pattern for every shell
    I toss upon the beach,
    I have a pattern for your life too.
    I really do, no matter how it
        looks
            or seems
                or feels
                    to you."

I looked at the handful of shells
    I had pocketed—
        the fluted white one,
        the spiraling color-banded one,
        the long thin spindled one—
    all so different, yet
    each with a perfect pattern.

As I held the designs,
the Designer held me
deep in His hand.
He caused me to see as He saw—
a pattern for every shell
scattered on the sands and
a pattern for me.

I heard His Word echoing within me:
"We are His workmanship,
    created in Christ Jesus
    unto good works,
    which God hath BEFORE ORDAINED
    that we should walk in them."

His sketch, His design for me
    predated time.

"Hear Me," He spoke again.
"As you look through your telescope
    the scene is blurred
    by the wrong focus—
    a focus on time.
"You are looking at your life as if
    time said it all,
    but I am preparing you
    for the endless reaches of
    eternity!
"In this world you had no choice
    over many lines in your pattern.
    You did not choose
    your era of birth,
    your country, family, social status.
    You did not choose
    your form, abilities, limitations.
    These I choose.

"But you ARE choosing your heavenly
    pattern.
    You will be rewarded or suffer loss
    as you invest the gifts and talents
    I have given you.

"Far more.
    As you choose to respond or react
    to the circumstances,
    to the people I send in life,
    you choose what you shall be
    and what you shall possess
    through all eternity.
    I have promised authority over cities
    to those who are faithful.
"Will you have two cities?
    Five?   Ten?

"Many in 'last place' here
    will be in 'first place' there.
    I make no mistake
    in the life that belongs to Me.
"Remember, you see only the dark beginnings,
    patterns that seem
        twisted
            marred
                broken.
    I plan for eternity."

Years earlier I had said:
"Lord,
I will believe what You say.
Jesus Christ died in my place,
for my sins.
Thank You for forgiving me.
Thank You for an eternal life
that begins right now."

This day He asked for another act of faith.
    Could I believe the Faithful One
    for another promise?
    "As for God, His way is perfect...
    He maketh my way—perfect."

Would I trust His pattern
    when I couldn't trace His design
    in the random—the nonsensical—
    the frustrating—the disappointing?
Would I believe He was fulfilling
    His eternal purpose in me?

I said, "Lord, I believe.
    I believe there is a pattern
    in the now.
    You are preparing me for the glory of
    eternity."

The beach remained the same.
    But now my telescope was focused.
    Looking at eternity, I saw
    life had meaning, destiny.

Exultant,
    I left the beach, recognizing that
    together
    God and I were fulfilling
    His eternal designs
    to His eternal glory.

Seasons later,
another parable...
The Parable of the

Tidepool

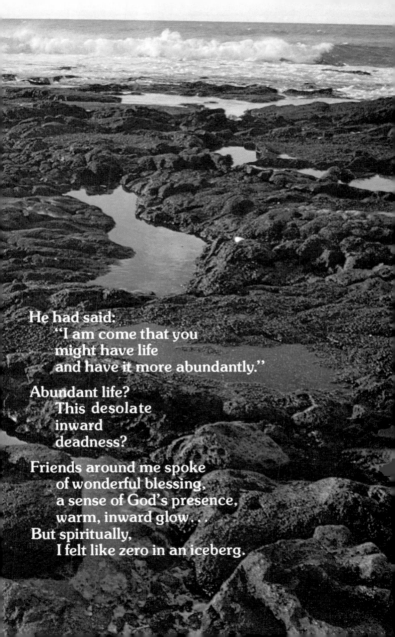

He had said:
"I am come that you
might have life
and have it more abundantly."

Abundant life?
This desolate
inward
deadness?

Friends around me spoke
of wonderful blessing,
a sense of God's presence,
warm, inward glow....
But spiritually,
I felt like zero in an iceberg.

A plan for life, yes,
    but a lifeless plan:
    The pattern was etched
    on a hollow shell.
Large areas of my disposition,
    my character,
    needed change—
    but nothing was happening.

Back to the beach I went
    in search of
    another shell,
    another message.

Surely God would bless EXACTLY as before.

But not one shell could I find
    on that long, long stretch
    of emptiness.
    Symbolic of my life!
    Not one shell on that beach
    to bless me.
    But I HAD to have a shell.
So I scrambled on over the rocks.

A tidepool!
  And there a shell at last—
  a rather ordinary shell,
  but at least a shell.
I reached in to pick it up,
  but it moved off.
  I reached for another
  and it scuttled away.
  The orange starfish wouldn't
  be moved;
  he was very much alive,
  clinging
  to a rock.
  The giant sea anemone contracted
  as I touched it.
  Tiny white-and-black-striped fish
  darted about.

I laughed.
I was looking to an empty shell
for blessing,
but God had led me
to inhabited shells,
to a pool that teemed with life . . .
to the Parable of the Tidepool.

God placed that pool right
    in the midst
    of the barren
        forsaken
        endless
        sand and rocks.
    Here where it seemed as if
    nothing was happening—
    no vital signs at all—
    He tucked away a pocket of life
    in a rock,
    a miniature ocean
    brimming
    with colorful creatures.

Did He have a tidepool in me?
    Could He invade my barrenness
    of spirit
    and bring forth vibrant life
    in me?
Could He bring changes
    in the sand and rocks
    of my disposition?

I knew how stubborn I was and
　　how unchangeable.
　　Like the starfish with his
　　thousand suction cups,
　　I clung
　　to the things of my choice.

The wind once again echoed His Word
　　to my heart:
　　"Now unto Him who is able to do
　　exceeding
　　abundantly above
　　all that we ask or think
　　according to the power that
　　worketh in us . . ."

A power working in me?
"Yes," He reminded.
　　"You received Me as your Saviour
　　and now I dwell within you
　　to reproduce MY own life.
　　I gave My life FOR you.
　　I give My life TO you.
　　I AM—IN you."

Would I believe that He,
    living within,
    could bring control to my temperament?
    Shift me off a self-centered anchorage?
    Transfuse and transform a self-willed,
    self-seeking person?

Would I trust Him to create moral beauty,
    to give desires for the right,
    to work out those desires into action?

I looked in the brilliantly clear pool
at this diverse display:
The neat, pin-striped fish,
the spiny, bright-purple sea urchin,
the responsive, flower-like anemone,
the hermit crab in his borrowed shell.
...Creator God.

He was saying, "Will you believe Me?
No matter how unproductive
the landscape of your life,
no matter how murky the waters?
I, the Creator of life
living within you,
will do exceeding abundantly...beyond
all you could ever ask...or dream."

His life in me! Pulsating life!
The risen, victorious life of Jesus Christ,
the greatest Power in the universe
effecting change in me.
I have the tidepool within!
"Lord, I believe.
I will depend on the power of that Life."

There was no surge of instant change.
I left the beach expectantly.
His life would be displayed
in me...the inhabited shell.

Years gone by
    and down by the sea,
    again at life's low tide...
The Parable of the Wave

I was standing this time upon a cliff,
    not searching,
    not expecting,
    just standing—looking—
    watching the movement of the sea,
    thinking back across some years,
    perplexed.

My work—perpetual empty motion, it seemed.
    The work and service of my friends
    was being used and blessed
    . . . mine was not.

No power, no dynamic, only movement;
    that was my life, my service.

Like the words of the Preacher:
    "The sun rises and the sun sets
    and breathlessly hurries
    to the place where it rises. . . .
    All the rivers flow to the sea
    but
    the sea is not full;
    to the place where the rivers flow,
    there they flow again."

I was taking on new work in a new city.
    People were depending on me.

"Wrong, Lord! Wrong time, wrong person."

"No," the gentle reply. "Right time,
    right person,
    wrong power."

Another reply, not gentle,
    exploding on the rocky cliff,
    receding,
    exploding again.
    Every crashing wave the voice
    of thunder:
    "All power is given
    unto Me
    in heaven and in earth,
    go therefore . . ."

God must sound it to my heart
    again and again
    as each wave,
    breaking with resonant authority,
    pounds the shore.

"The power, the glory is Mine.
    You do My bidding and
    I will use you as I choose."

Mine were eyes turned inward,
    eyes ever looking
    where power could never be.

He turned them to the coastline below
    to see His power in the
    Parable of the Waves.

In the distant cove these twilight waves
    were gentle on the sand,
    waves serenely molding
    a mighty coastline,
    shaping the borders
    of a nation.

On the beach, great logs had been tossed
    by the power of the waves
    and strewn like matchsticks.

Off shore, a sunset tableau of huge rocks
    had been sculptured by wind
    and those same waves.

I climbed down the cliff to walk the beach;
the power of the sea
continued to speak to me.

Sand underfoot gave way in places to
    carved rocks, deeply
    carved by the ebbing
    and flowing tide.
Even gently lapping, ever in and out,
    the sea demonstrated unremitting
    power.

Farther along, the fury of the waves,
    booming as they broke,
    had hewn a large cave out
    of a rock-faced bluff.

I held the sea water in my hand.
    It had no energy of its own
    to do anything large or small.
    The energy was not in the water
    but in the waves.

On the horizon, the water—
    a placid,
    mirrored surface—
    hid the turbulence caused by
    great wave trains,
    pulses of pure energy,
    skimming the ocean,
    powering orbiting water masses
    which crest and break
    in the shallows.

Hammering the rocks,
    a wave tossed
    a spectacular burst of flying spray.
Breaking on the beach,
    it gently spread a white edge
    of sparkling foam bubbles.

However displayed,
    the power of the waves is invincible,
    ever changing
    the contour of the coast,
    the profile of the beach.

As I looked at the water in my hands
    and at the waves,
    the Lord reminded me,
    "Forget what YOU are.
    You, like the water,
    are without one ounce of power—
    not even one.
ALL power is given unto ME."

Once again, would I believe God?
Would I really expect
    HIM
    to accomplish miracles through
    me,
    an ordinary person,
    an ordinary life,
    in ordinary surroundings?

With His power,
 He would like to accomplish
 great things through me,
 using me
 to mold others by my influence,
 to change the direction
 of the coastline in some lives,
 to shape surroundings for Him—
 gently or firmly,
 to lift great logs of guilt
 or worry
 from shoulders,
 to make safe caves for those who need
 comfort from storms.

All this, He would do through His power in me
 in my every day walk.

Even as I stood there,
   I found myself limiting Him
   by thinking
   that with my ordinary abilities
   I must not expect TOO much.

Once again, He said, "I couldn't care less
   what water this wave is made of.
   I am the One who supplies the power.
   Will you believe that
   I will do
   what I say?"

Again, the question, "Will you,
   like a child,
   simply believe Me?"

The shell
   the tidepool
      and now the waves . . .

I had known the Scriptures.
   But knowing is never enough.
   God asked for something more.

Reaching up, I whispered the words again:
   "Lord Jesus, I BELIEVE You."

I left the beach
   confidently.

Three times the Promiser had spoken . . .
His pattern for me,
His pulsating life in me,
His power through me.
God's flood tide!